PASSWORDS

7 Steps to Writing a Memorable Eulogy

CYRUS M. COPELAND

For my Dad, whom I still miss.

Delivering his eulogy started me on this journey.

Also by Cyrus M. Copeland

FAREWELL, GODSPEED: The Greatest Eulogies of
Our Time.

A WONDERFUL LIFE: 50 Eulogies to Lift the Spirit.

OFF THE RADAR: A Father's Secret, A Mother's Heroism,
and a Son's Quest.

Do not stand at my grave and weep
I am not there, I do not sleep
I am the thousand winds that blow
I am the diamond glints in the snow
I am the sunlight on ripened grain
I am a gentle autumn's rain
When you awaken in the morning hush
I am the swift uplifting rush
I am the birds in circled flight
I am the soft stars that shine at night
So do not stand on my grave and cry
I am not there
I did not die.

—*Melinda Sue Pacho*

Contents

Introduction

A decade ago, I delivered my father's eulogy. Talk to anyone who has delivered a eulogy and they'll tell you this: It is a cathartic and connective experience. Through the tears, I was gratified to have done it.

Afterward, I had the idea to organize a book of eulogies for our cultural heroes—a kind of front-row seat at their memorials. To my surprise there were no such books. So I did what we all do with those occasional flashes of creative inspiration: Nothing. I went back to my job in advertising and cushy expense account and submitted to the humdrum life of Madison Avenue, selling everything from cough drops to cars.

But I am a New Yorker and in the days after 9/11, life changed. I couldn't leave my apartment without passing a church and hearing one, two, five eulogies a day to fallen firemen, policemen, these newfound American heroes, and suddenly the idea to do a collection of eulogies to our heroes was rekindled. I left my advertising job. I got an agent and publishing deal in surprisingly short order. And I dedicated myself to studying the art of remembrance.

After *Farewell, Godspeed* was published, life changed. Funny thing about death, it gives new life to those left behind. I finally had a much dreamt about literary career. I was giving interviews to *The New York Times* and the like, chatting up funeral directors, guesting on radio shows. But mostly I remember this: Being struck by the unexpected beauty of this art form and the vulnerability implicit in it: Will we be well remembered? Will we be seen and recognized for who are? Will we be known?

You know that part in the movies where everything rests on the shoulders of a buckling hero? It's the eleventh hour. Will he gather the threads of narrative, and weave them into something important—something bigger, which doesn't just save the damsel but also assert his humanity and render him a unique man, different from all the heroes which preceded him? So it is with the eulogy. Our hero has died, but his humanity hangs in the balance: Will we recognize him in these words?

The New Goodbye

"We are always saying farewell in this world, always standing the edge of loss attempting to retrieve some memory, some human meaning from the silence, something which is precious and gone." Adlai Stevenson spoke these words at Eleanor Roosevelt's memorial. In doing so, he captured both the poignant nature of life and the challenge of eulogizing—how to retrieve something from the silence?

The eulogy has a long history and strange reputation. From Pericles' Funeral Oration in Athens, to Lincoln's Gettysburg Address, to Earl Spencer's scandalous and riveting farewell for Princess Di, to the remembrance I delivered for my dad, the eulogy goes on. A century ago, eulogies were orations—longwinded and unequaled in their capacity to induce torpor. Listen to Reverend Beecher's eulogy for Ulysses S. Grant: "Another name is added to the roll of those whom the world will not willingly let die. A few years since storm clouds filled his heaven and slander and bitter lies rained down on him. The clouds are all blown away, under a serene sky he laid down his life, and the Nation wept." Xanax, anyone? Thankfully, the modern eulogy is light on melodrama and much more celebratory. It lifts the spirit and tells stories. It is honest. It focuses on the life of the departed instead of the loss of the gathered.

And it is about the human life, not the Afterlife. As recently as a couple decades ago, 90% of eulogies were delivered by priests, who loaded their goodbyes with psalms and stories of salvation, which frankly had little bearing on the life of the departed. But something happened in the past few years that expanded the art form into something much more democratic and personal.

Today it's people like you and I stepping up to the podium to remember our lovers, friends, mentors, teachers and parents. When Princess Diana's funeral was broadcast around the world, it wasn't the Archbishop of Canterbury eulogizing her, it was her brother. To these shifting cultural sands add: self empowered youth, the transient American family unknown to their clergy, the unrehearsed sensibility of reality TV—all have conspired to put us behind the podium. Only without a direct line to the Divine, will our eulogies still inspire?

Because this is the uncomfortable truth: The eulogy combines our two biggest fears, death and public speaking, *at the same time.*

Building Bridges

Here is a handbook on delivering an inspired and loving goodbye, distilled down to seven steps. Not a writer? Don't worry, this book will teach you how to wade into memory and step forward with what you've found. When I set out to compose my father's eulogy, I could hear his voice in my head telling me that this wasn't a sad occasion. And I knew that somehow he was *there* in a different, non-imaginary way. I knew it. It was a kind of bridge that stretched across the chasm of his absence in my life.

And that is what a good eulogy can be: A bridge between the living and the dead, between *us* and *them*, memory and eternity, my memories of my dad and a lifetime that stretches forward without him. A great eulogy assures us that our loved ones will endure in our collective memories. The more specific and real the remembrances, the stronger the bridge.

"There may be little or much beyond the grave," Robert Frost wrote, "but the strong are saying nothing 'til they see."

Frost was wrong. Miked and suited and taking the floor, the strong are saying plenty.

You'll see.

Thinking

———————— •◦●◦• ————————

How to begin? I like to start with a prayer, tea, an easy chair––feel free to pick your own nourishments. Quiet helps. So does caffeine. It kicks my heart and mind into action, helps me make interesting connections, and sensitizes me to the beauty of life. As a writer, I would rather do almost anything than write––throw in the prospect of writing a *eulogy* and that is especially true. But surrounded by these comforts, I feel strong enough to give myself over to sorrow.

There is something about the entwining of sorrow and memory that yields a powerful alloy. It's why goodbyes hit hard. Why the first letter you write after a break-up brims with beauty. Why the eulogy is a powerful art form. Because as Kahlil Gibran says, "And ever has it been that love knows not of its own depth until the hour of separation."

10 Questions to Get You Started

Think of your eulogy as a story. Every good story begins with a question, a search for what is true. Here are ten questions to spark your muses.

1. "I remember when …" What are the keenest memories you have of your loved one? Sometimes the thing that floats right to the surface is also the most powerful. When my father died, I immediately thought of the day he took me and my sister to a valley—a memory which carried forward 20 years, and remains a defining moment in my life.

2. What was the last thing you said to them? The last thing you wish you'd said?

3. Conversely, "The first time I met …"

4. When were they happiest?

5. What are the highlights of their life story? Think of your loved one at different ages, and in different roles. Employee, spouse, friend, churchgoer, etc. Don't just think big here, think small too. What were their habits and foibles and surrounding stories? Details count.

6. What is your favorite story to tell about them?

7. What made them special? Not just favorite pastimes, likes and dislikes, but what was unique to their soul? The answer to this question will set your eulogy apart. Part of my father's mission was to open the eyes of others to the beauty of small things. And so he would occasionally bring home an autumn leaf and leave it on

the pillow of my mother, who was eternally perplexed at his choice of gifts.

8. If I could say only three things about them, what would it be? Start with their deepest belief.

9. What did their favorite song reveal about their soul?

10. What is the most important thing you learned from them?

Frequently, deciding *what* to say is harder than deciding how to say it. Fortunately, this is neither a biography nor obituary; you don't have to winnow down their entire life. The eulogy is a personal, post mortem toast. Your first order of business is to decide which aspects of your loved one to focus on.

These are ten of about a thousand questions that reveal character. For the moment, do nothing but enjoy the answers to these questions—they are the residue of a well lived life. Memories will lead to other memories. Feast on them. Reflect.

Sip your tea.

Writing: 7 Steps to a Memorable Eulogy

━━━━●━◆━●◆●●━●━━━━

Now let's take these details of a life and put them into form. Try this one of two ways: If you're feeling full and sensitive and creative right now, give into it. *Dive* into it. Don't worry about structure—just write and see where it goes. We all have muses who are there to inspire us in moments like this, and now would be a good time to turn the reigns over to them. Good writing, good art, good music—great artists will tell you that the interesting stuff happens when you just let go, surrender to feeling and inspiration and *let it flow*.

As for the rest of us—the vast majority who've never delivered a eulogy? We need a little help with structure.

BLUEPRINTS

Most people like to outline their speeches—ensuring not just a flow of thought, but focus. An outline is like blueprints for a house. A foundation to build on and return to if/when you get lost in the process. When I composed my grandmother's eulogy, her highly individualistic character came to mind: strong and stubborn, she was nothing like her name 'Dolly'. That

9

inconsistency was a place to begin—and it gave me a theme to organize the eulogy around. Look over 10 Questions. The interesting answers will point you in a direction. Once you decide on a theme, the thoughts will begin to flow, memories and stories come to mind, each feeding freely upon the other– at which point you should jot them down. *This outline will be the skeletal structure of your eulogy.* This isn't high school English, your outline needn't follow a particular form, but it does need to be concise. Put your points and stories in order. Above all, keep it simple—no longer than a page.

Edith Freundlich was a fascinating woman whose life was a dance with Death begun in a concentration camp half a century ago. It was a relationship longer than all the others, and when she finally succumbed to it, her son saw that ending as a place to begin. Here's the outline of his eulogy for Edith:

Introduction and theme: Edith's bond with Death

    a.   Concentration camp

Death's successor: Love

    a.   Husband

    b.   Younger brother

    c.   Grandchildren

Edith's character and stories

    a.   Devotion to memory

    b.   Well known vanity

    c.   Last e-mail from Edith

Conclusion

    a.   Description of death scene

    b.   Reunion with Death—bookending eulogy

To see how he builds a powerful goodbye from these simple blueprints, turn to page 90 where I've reprinted his eulogy. I love how he introduces the theme up front and returns to it like a master storyteller, allowing us the satisfaction of a story arc. Above all, observe how an outline is simply a collection of points to expand upon, nothing more.

Having made my way through hundreds of farewells, I've noticed what the best ones have in common—distilled down to seven simple steps. After you've finished this section, you will have a clear understanding of how to structure and write a memorable eulogy.

Here are the seven keystones to a great goodbye.

1.   START STRONG

Journalists will tell you: Hook 'em with a lead.

Do *not* begin 'We are gathered here today to…" The dearly beloved know why they're there. When Madonna eulogized Gianni Versace, she began, "I slept in Gianni Versace's bed" and, true to form, she had our attention as soon as she opened her mouth.

Winona Ryder began her farewell to godfather Timothy Leary, "Three months after I was born, my dad went to see Tim in Switzerland, where he was living in exile after escaping prison and beings called 'the most dangerous man in the world' by Nixon, who was furiously trying to hunt him down."

Lincoln wrestled for hours before coming up with these six words: "Four score and seven years ago…"

Diane Sawyer on Lucille Ball: "There is a debate that is one of the longest-running theological arguments in Christianity. A debate that has engaged everybody from dusty old scholars in the Medieval Ages to Baudelaire. The issue is this: Is there laughter in heaven?"

Be bold. A strong beginning gives the audience notice—sit up and pay attention—and gives you confidence. Speaking powerful words, we feel empowered. Consider beginning with a story about the deceased. Or the last thing they said to you. Or the deceased's first name, which is a simple and powerful way to begin. You want a foundation strong enough to build the rest of your eulogy on.

20 GREAT OPENERS

The children of fighter pilots tell different stories than other kids do. None of our fathers can write a will or sell a life insurance policy or fill out a prescription or administer a flu shot or explain what a poet meant. We tell of fathers who land on aircraft carriers at pitch-black night with the wind howling out of the China Sea. —*Pat Conroy on his father, Don "The Great Santini" Conroy*

To give the funeral of Dr. Martin Luther King, Jr. is like eulogizing one's deceased son, so close and so precious was he to me. — *Benjamin Mays on Martin Luther King*

I think of this as a reunion. My mother first met death a long time ago, at a couple of concentration camps in Germany. The two of them spent every minute together for months, were intimate in unimaginable ways, shared a wooden shelf at night and what little there was to eat, or, more often, went hungry together for days, trudged about in the cold and mud, became a single being almost — and then, finally, parted company. Death decided — to her everlasting amazement — that although it wanted a great many others she knew and loved, and millions more she knew about but had never met, it did not, after all that, want her. This puzzled and angered her forever. — *Peter Freundlich on Edith Freundlich*

Besides celebrating Andy Warhol as the quintessential artist of his time, I'd like to recall a side of his character that he hid from all but his closest friends: his spiritual side. — *John Richardson on Andy Warhol*

On the 14th of March at a quarter to three in the afternoon, the greatest living thinker ceased to think. — *Friendrich Engels on Karl Marx*

One week ago in the Rose Garden at Hyde Park, Eleanor Roosevelt came home for the last time. Her journeys are over. The remembrance now begins.— *Adlai Stevenson on Eleanor Roosevelt*

About 14 years ago, I was hiding behind a potted plant and this girl asked if I could help her be a parakeet, and I've been smitten with Gilda ever since. — *Alan Zweibel on Gilda Radner*

I shall always remember the life of James Dean as a drama in three acts. — *Rev. Xen Harvey on James Dean*

You had to be on your toes around Jack Lemmon. If only to get a glimpse of how high his standards were. — *Larry Gelbart on Jack Lemmon*

We have been friends together. But it is a new year and a new time, and we are to be together in a new way. — *John Culkin on Marshall McLuhan*

When they told me they were going to induct my friend George Harrison in the Hollywood Bowl Hall of Fame posthumously, my first thought was, I bet he won't show up. — *Eric Idle on George Harrison*

We are all mortal. So it had to happen. Ted Geisel had to leave this earth sometime. — *Robert Bernstein on Dr. Seuss*

Once when they asked John what he would do if he was elected president, he said, 'I guess the first thing is call up

Uncle Teddy and gloat.' I loved that. It was so like his father. — *Ted Kennedy on JFK Jr.*

Lenny Bruce's death was no more untimely or uncalled for than the attacks upon his life and livelihood by an indignant society. He tore the skin off every phony reaction in this human existence of ours. — *Rev. Howard Moody on Lenny Bruce*

A wise man told me the most a person can say about his or her life is, "I was here! I mattered!" Well, goodness knows, Bette Davis was here. And she mattered. — *David Hartman on Bette Davis*

I stand before you today the representative of a family in grief, in a county in mourning, before a world in shock. — *Earl Spencer on Princess Diana*

I know it sounds off, but somehow I did not believe Joan Crawford could ever die. She was the perfect image of a movie star, and as such largely the creation of her own indomitable will. — *George Cukor on Joan Crawford*

The untimely death of a beautiful woman is one of the oldest romantic conventions in art and literature, from Hamlet's Ophelia to some of the real-life models chosen by the pre-Raphaelite painters to Poe's Annabel Lee. These women, whether real or fictional, died for art or for love. Marilyn Monroe died for neither. — *Donald Spoto on Marilyn Monroe*

For being the legendary expert on death and dying she was the most alive person I have ever met. — *David Kessler on Elisabeth Kübler Ross*

2. THE MIDDLE PART: GET PERSONAL

It's easy to hide behind words and platitudes, talk about the Afterlife instead of the human life, or, worse, say nondescript things like "Aunt Mary was a lovely person." (Yawn.) A eulogy is not One Size Fits All, and it is not an obituary. Races run? Promotions? Awards? Leave that to the newspapers and give your audience an intimate look at Mary. Think of your eulogy as a toast to the deceased. This means you can draw aside the curtain of decorum and be personal. Remembrances? Acts of kindness? Favorite 2AM moments? Stories told? Gifts that changed the trajectory of your life? All are fair game.

One option: Write a letter to the deceased—thus skirting the traditional structure of a speech, and fooling your mind into thinking you're talking to one person instead of dozens. Infinitely more personal. There are no boundaries here, except of course decorum. This isn't the time for recriminations, but it might be the time to give voice to things you were too shy or too late to say? Perhaps things you learned from them? Or how they changed your life? Freed from the structural confines of a speech, a letter to an old friend is easy, and your audience will remember its intimacy.

Either way, remember, this is a eulogy and not an obituary pulled from the *New York Times* vault. *Make it personal.*

Larry Gelbart offers this cautionary tale about professional eulogizer George Jessel:

"Sprinkling kudos, Jessel would heap encomiums upon his subjects by the shovelful, however crude the analogy. So frequent were his stand-ups alongside those who were lying down, it was rumored Jessel could be compensated for his compassion; that his praise could be bought by the pound. And why not? Whereas his income had been greatly diminished when vaudeville died, mortality never has shown the slightest sign of going out of business.Bolstering the suspicion that his empathy might indeed have had a price tag attached, was the instance in which Jessel, extolling the virtues of the encased gentleman with whom he was sharing the stage, praised the man's excellence as a husband, as a father, a patriot, a philanthropist nonpareil, making his subject sound as though he was eligible for instant elevation to sainthood. Enraptured by his own eloquence, almost airsick from the loftiness of his prose, Jessel paused a moment, lowered his eyes and gazed at the open coffin. Shocked by a sudden realization, he looked out at the assembled and announced: 'My God, I know this man.'"

Ouch.

What if you didn't know the deceased well enough to speak personally? One solution is to talk about the larger themes of their life. As a New Yorker, I'll always remember the eulogies delivered for 9/11 heroes—among them Capt. Frank Callahan's. Firemen don't sit around talking about dreams and hopes; they're a rough and tumble bunch that give testosterone a good name. Because his colleague didn't know Callahan well, he spoke professionally about the brotherhood and duties which bound firemen—so movingly that *The New York Times* reprinted his farewell word for word, as I have done at the end of this book. It is a stunning eulogy. It is one of the rare times that a professional perspective trumps the personal.

Getting personal is often a challenge for clergy. How do you say something personal about someone you don't know well, especially in denominations like the Catholic church, where a priest oversees a congregation that can number in the thousands?

One way to get personal is to…

3. TELL TALES

Stories illustrate character. Instead of telling us that Aunt Mary was an inveterate talker, show us. Are phone calls with her so one-sided that you can put the phone down, make a turkey sandwich, and return without missing a beat? Stories bring the dearly departed to life for one last time. When James Woods eulogized Bette Davis, he recounted this story:

> *Life* magazine approached me and said, "You have been chosen by Miss Davis to be the actor she'd most like to be photographed with, as the great stars of 1939 pose with some new young actors." I was honored. So we were posing for Greg Gorman, and she looked great— with the same presence she always had and a little bit more. Greg said, "If you would sit there, and Miss Davis, could you just put your hand on his shoulder."
>
> She looks over to him and says, "I think *not.*"
>
> "Is there a problem?"
>
> "This young man is betrothed, I don't want to cause any problems."
>
> Greg came over to me and said, "She's kidding right?" And I said, "No. I grew up in Rhode Island and she's from Connecticut. She knows one woman does not paw another woman's man."

Greg says, "But she is quite a bit older. I don't think she's a threat."

"Well, *she* thinks she's a threat and I have to tell you, there's quite a bit of woman there. I think probably Miss Davis will always be a threat in that area." A great woman has a power to move and to pain and to beguile, and she's always been aware of that. But eventually she put her hand on my shoulder and we got the shot. It was okay because she was seduced into it. She wasn't responsible.

See how a story lets us take a break from the unrelenting formality of the moment? A good tale illustrates character, takes the audience down a side road, reminds them this is a celebration of life. It says we left an imprint. And in the case of Miss Davis, that her eighty-year-old ego was quite healthy, thanks. So tell tales, even irreverent ones. No one is going to think you're self-centered just because you recount a few stories in the first person.

4. LAUGH A LITTLE

Life is funny—there's no reason that a celebration of their life should approximate Dostoevsky. Humor lessens the tension! (Especially yours.) The quick victory of laughter will bond you and your audience, helping them to relax, get comfortable and settle into their chairs.

When Bob Fosse died, funnyman Neil Simon eulogized him with a Ten Best Moments of Bob Fosse's life.

> Moment #3: "The opening night of *Little Me* in New York. I was standing with Bob and Cy Coleman at the back of the house and Sid Caesar, who otherwise gave a brilliant performance, coughed on each of his first three laugh lines—causing, obviously, no one to laugh on his first three laugh lines. I looked at Cy, Cy looked at me and then we both looked at Bob. Bob very simply put his arms down at his sides, closed his eyes, and fell backwards, every part of his body hitting the floor simultaneously—a perfect Ten at any Olympics. He hardly moved on the floor, except to moan very quietly. And then a few minutes later, a very hostile and inebriated man got out of his seat, walked up the aisle on his way to the men's room, turned to us and said angrily, "This is the worst goddamned show I've seen since *My Fair Lady*." Bob laughed until he cried."

Like the concept of a Ten Best Moments eulogy? Feel free to poach. It makes a good excuse to collect vignettes from family members who will appreciate your weaving their memories into your eulogy. Focus on a common theme for the stories, or assign everyone difference eras from the deceased's life, or else your remembrance might sound like a hodgepodge of disconnected thoughts.

Bob Newhart observed, "laughter gives us distance. It allows us to step back from an event, deal with it and move on." Laughter through the tears is the most powerful—allowing us to hold the contradiction of loss alongside laughter, then transcend both. So go ahead. It's a eulogy, but you can still tell a funny story.

5. BE HONEST

People aren't gathered to see someone canonized, and can smell a pile of, uh, insincerity from a mile away. There is a way to be truthful without being disrespectful. Listen to Bob Hope on Jack Benny: "He was eternally stingy. He gave us only 80 years and it wasn't enough."

This is the thing about honesty: It allows us to remember the deceased for the person they were, rather than the saint no one recognizes. Does any really care that Bob Fosse was a womanizer? Or that Jack Benny was a cheapskate? We forgive their lapses, knowing any trace of judgment has been sideswiped by the gentle laugh of recognition.

Death has a way of making us less judgmental, transmuting flaws into proof of humanity. Earl Spencer on Princess Diana: "For all the status, the glamour, the applause, Diana remained throughout a very insecure person at heart, almost childlike in her desire to do good for others so she could release herself from deep feelings of unworthiness, of which her eating disorders were merely a symptom." Having lionized his sister, he now humanizes her—drawing us even closer. A single line is all it takes. (Seriously. You can stop after the second foible—after that, it's only piling on.) Honesty is like Botox. A little goes a long way.

When Bill Murray eulogized his agent Jay Maloney, he surveyed the auditorium full of Hollywood producers and directors and began, "Looking around me, I see many people I would rather be eulogizing today." He went on to identify a few such people––leaving his audience in sidesplitting laughter because he is Bill Murray and can get away with outrageous pronouncements.

How honest should you be? If the circumstances surrounding death were violent or tragic, say, should you acknowledge then? After Kurt Cobain's suicide, Courtney Love read his suicide note in lieu of a eulogy—punctuated with exclamations of anger, love, and several choice expletives. When I came upon her goodbye, I wept. It was the most honest eulogy I'd read. It was not gracious or uplifting. It was coarse and impassioned and a tear-stained, exactly what you'd expect considering the source. And you should *not* construe this as a recommendation to substitute ranting for reflection, dear reader. But candor has its place. It brings us onto common ground. It liberates. It draws the thread connecting us all tighter. It says we are strong enough to face the truth together.

6. BIG MOMENTS

Into every life, transcendent moments land. When this happens the spirit lifts and life changes.

An instant from my own childhood: My father had taken my sister and me to a valley in Iran overrun with creeks and chlorophyll and berries and partridge, and for an afternoon taught us the beauty of small things. Autumn air cleaved with frost that burnt in the lungs. Circular gold leaves that shimmered like coins. The taste of peanut butter after hours of trekking. Those were the lessons of my childhood that no one but my father—my world-gallivanting, nature-loving, observant, educator of a father—could have taught.

When I turned 30, I decided to return to the valley of my youth. "Draw me a map?" I asked him. My father refused. "Let the valley live in memory." I insisted; I am a stubborn Taurus son. He drew a map on the back of an envelope, then a couple months later, died.

When I returned to Iran, I was dismayed to discover that everything was undersized and out of proportion. Surveying my childhood home and school, I felt like Gulliver in Lilliput. And I'd lost the envelope my father inscribed, but somehow found my way back to the valley—only to discover that the valley was *larger* than I recalled. It had grown up. The poplar trees now brushed the sky and the meandering creeks had joined, morphing into a raging river so deep, so wide, Vasco De Gama might have reversed course. The beauty of small things was nowhere to be found. But the scent? Fecund with a tinge of autumnal decay, that was the scent of the best day of my life— and with it everything else came rushing back. Traipsing across hill and dale, I realized: Nothing ever stays the same, nothing, but if you're lucky, the people and places you love will grow alongside you. My father had died long before I got a chance to revisit the valley, but traversing its untamed beauty I could swear that he was there too, a light but undeniable presence. He too had shifted form.

If you can come up with a Big Moment, consider yourself lucky and see if you can't organize your eulogy around it. There is something not just truthful, but universal, hidden in its folds.

Big moments show perspective. As FDNY Champlain, Father Mychal Judge was responsible for tending to the firefighter's soul, and accompanied his men on a fateful call to duty. He was the first man pulled from the rubble of 9/11. "There are between two and three hundred firemen buried at Ground Zero, his eulogizer noted. "But Mychal is going to be on the other side of death to greet them instead of sending them there. He's going to greet them with that big Irish smile, take them by the arm and say, 'Welcome, I want to take you to my Father.' He can continue doing in death what he couldn't do in life." His eulogy was among the first attempts to reach into the heart of such a vast, sprawling tragedy and extract something purposeful. If that's not a Big Moment, I don't know what is.

Big Moments can be philosophical. Question God and you've got a built-in Big Moment. Alan Zweibel on Gilda Radner: "I don't know why God makes people and then takes them back while they're still having fun with the life he gave them in the first place. Just like I don't know if I'm supposed to celebrate the fact that Gilda was in my life, or feel cheated that she's not here anymore. But even though her body grew to betray her, spirits just don't die..."

A Big Moment can also be this moment. Pat Conroy at the funeral of The Great Santini—whose cinematic funeral had already been shot: "You will be witnessing the actual burial that has already been filmed in a fictional setting. This has never happened in world history. You will be present in a scene that was acted out in film in 1979. You will be in the same small town and the same cemetery. Only the Great Santini himself will be different."

The one thing Big Moments have in common? Drama. Was there an 'aha' moment that stood out? A time when the deceased fought the good fight? Or an instant when her soul cracked open? A big moment isn't the same as a grandiose moment, which is best left for soap operas and Busby Berkley musicals, but it is dramatic so think big. Give us goose bumps. Mine the drama of the deceased's life and tell the truth—the higher truth—about life, love, and the imprint on the world they left behind.

7. CLOSE WELL

It's goodbye! Send your dearly departed into the afterlife on a powerful updraft. James Woods delivered this classic closer at Bette Davis's memorial: "Fasten your seatbelts, it's going to be a bumpy eternity."

Other memorable parting shots:

Robert Ingersoll on Walt Whitman: "And so I lay this little wreath on this great man's tomb. I loved him living, and I love him still."

Ossie Davis on Malcolm X: "What we place in the ground is no more now a man, but a seed which after the winter of our discontent will come forth again to meet us. And we will know him then for what he was and is—a prince, our own, black, shining prince!—who didn't hesitate to die because he loved us so."

Madonna on Gianni Versace: "I'm going to miss you, Gianni. We're all going to miss you. But I've got a pocketful of memories in my Versace jeans, and they're not going anywhere."

You may want to close with the last thing you said to them—or wanted to say? Dan Aykroyd concluded his eulogy for John Belushi by cranking up *The 2000 Pound Bee* and somewhere, Belushi tipped his fedora in recognition. Many a eulogist has closed with a poem. Check out the selection in the next chapter.

Whatever you choose, it's the final valediction, so make it count.

---

20 GREAT PARTING SHOTS

I can see her sharing a platter of oysters and a cold bottle of wine with Escoffier. And now that she has joined him, the food will be commensurably better in heaven. — *Jacques Pépin on Julia Child*

I just hope God has a place for him where he can run again. Where he can play practical jokes on his teammates and smile that boyish smile, 'cause God knows, no one's perfect. And God knows there's something special about heroes. So long, Mick. Thanks. — *Bob Costas on Mickey Mantle*

I thought Joan Crawford could never die. Come to think of it, as long as celluloid holds together and the world Hollywood means anything to anyone, she never will. — *George Cukor on Joan Crawford*

Her special talent was this: She could sing so that it would break your heart. What is a tough audience? A tough audience is a group of high income bracket cynics at a Hollywood party. Judy's gift to them was to wring tears from men with hearts of rock. — *James Mason on Judy Garland*

She was once asked her goal in life. "I just want to be wonderful," she replied quietly. And so you were, Marilyn. And so you were. — *Donald Spoto on Marilyn Monroe*

I will miss her beyond words and I am happy for her; and so relieved that she is no longer confined to a body, or confined to a bed or confined to even this world. Elisabeth was always too big to be contained. — *David Kessler on Elisabeth Kübler Ross*

Sometimes I wake up in the early morning from a dream and think that I can see her there in the room with me. I think that she stays around for those first few seconds after waking to let me know that she is watching me. And that she is waiting for me to let my own light shine. I love you Mother. — *Michael Meadows on Karen Silkwood*

Semper Fi, Dad. Semper Fi, O Great Santini. — *Pat Conroy on Don Conroy*

I feel your silent laughter
at sentiments so bold
that dare to step across the line
to tell what must be told,
so I'll just say I love you,
which I never said before
and let it go at that old friend
the rest you may ignore.
— *Robert Hunter on Jerry Garcia*

What lies ahead for Cy's music is an eternity of replays, a never ending, perpetual reprise of his songs right up until the moment this planet cools and shrinks to the size of an eighth note. — *Larry Gelbart on Cy Coleman*

Above all, we give thanks for the life of a woman I am so proud to be able to call my sister – the unique, the complex, the extraordinary and irreplaceable Diana, whose beauty, both internal and external, will never be extinguished from our minds. — *Earl Spencer on Princess Diana*

A nation, too, will long feel the loss of her seven sons and daughters, her seven good friends. We can find consolation only in faith, for we know in our hearts that you who flew so high and so proud now make your home beyond the stars, safe in God's promise of eternal life. — *President Reagan on Challenger Astronauts*

Fatherland or death, we shall win! — *Fidel Castro on Che Guevara*

Even as an adult, she was still a little girl who believed in fairy tales and that if she said "Bunny Bunny" on the first day of every month, it would bring her love, laughter and peace. Well, Gilda, this is June 1st and if you're in a place where you can't say it, I'll say it for you. "Bunny Bunny" and I hope you're okay. I'm gonna miss you, Gilbert. — *Alan Zweibel on Gilda Radner*

She graced our history. And for those of us who knew and loved her – she graced our lives. — *Senator Kennedy on Jackie Onassis*

The career of James Dean has not ended, it has just begun. And remember, God Himself is directing the production. — *Rev. Xen Harvey on James Dean*

We dared to think, in that other Irish phrase, that this John Kennedy would live to comb gray hair, with his beloved Carolyn by his side. But like his father, he had every gift but length of years. — *Senator Ted Kennedy on JFK Jr.*

You have given us this anger to remember and to use in a bad world. We thank you, we honor you, and we all say goodbye to you now with a love that should calm that anger of yours forever. — *William Styron on Lillian Hellman*

As he said many times, Some men see things as they are and say why. I dream of things that never were and say whey not? — *Senator Ted Kennedy on Robert Kennedy*

With God's help and each of yours, we'll make AIDS a disease and not a dirty word. — *Rev. Ray Probasco on Ryan White*

In Sum...

1. Start strong
2. Get personal
3. Tell stories
4. Be honest
5. Use humor
6. Include a big moment
7. Close well

That's it. These are the tools for a great goodbye. And now that you have them, the great work begins—it's time to put your thoughts into form. After deciding what to say, writing is the second hardest part. Talk to writers, the honest ones will confess their procrastination techniques honed to crystalline perfection. (Cleaning is mine; hey, at least I'm doing *something*.) But since you're not a professional writer, put down this book and get to work. Go! It's been lovely spending this time together—but the cover price only gets you a smart guidebook. Writers not included.

But first... maybe just *one* more cup of tea?

Polishing

———————— ◆◆◆◆◆ ————————

Write first. Edit afterward. Do yourself a favor and remember that—else you'll still be at the keyboard while the mourners are filing in. Writing requires freedom of spirit. Editing requires perfectionism. Those two are opposing forces, constantly doing battle. Trying to write and edit will likely drive your muses away and leave you exasperated, fistfuls of hair strewn across your computer. Don't comb thesauruses for the perfect word. Don't stop to fix spelling. Be judgmental only when you start to edit—judgmental and picky and everything you'd expect from your mother-in-law. But not while you're writing, got it? The first draft is never perfect.

When you're finally finished, do three things: (1) put aside the eulogy, (2) puff up your chest and take stock in your accomplishment, then (3) go pick out your funeral outfit. Only when you return should you begin the process of editing, at which points the flaws will positively leap off the page. Herewith, some tips to help you cope:

How Long?

There is no set rule of thumb—most eulogies last between 5 and 15 minutes. A 10-minute speech is about 5 typed pages long, double-spaced.

Be Merciless

Fall in love with a phrase of paragraph you wrote that just doesn't fit? Cut it. The same applies to any extra words—cut, cut, cut. With a powerful eulogy, less is emphatically more. Eliminate every last superfluous, needless, unnecessary, gratuitous word.

Do I Write It Word for Word?

If it helps. Most of us write in a different voice than we speak, so make sure it doesn't sound stilted. If you're feeling confident, jot down your key points on a card and speak from that.

Be Yourself

Easier once you realize this isn't about you, it's about the person in the casket or urn. The audience is there to pay homage and indulge in the camaraderie of collective sadness—not to judge you. The most comforting thing you can do for them is to be yourself.

Vary Sentence Length

This helps establish a rhythm to the eulogy—short bursts, longer stretches of prose, short bursts. Your eulogy will sound more pleasing to the ear and hold your audience's attention.

Speak assertively

Don't hedge. "Mary's wisdom cut to the bone," sounds a lot better than "On occasion, some of us experienced Mary's keen intellect." And since you're not giving a lecture at Oxford, speak simply!

Speaking

———————•◦●◦•———————

George Jessel once noted the human brain starts working the moment you're born and never stops until you stand up to speak in public—cold comfort from a man who delivered hundreds of eulogies. Happily, mourners aren't critics. They just want something that is truthful and if it gives them some perspective, a story, a few laughs in a dark moment, they're grateful for the balm. Here are a few tips for delivering your farewell.

1. Look good. Used to be everyone dressed in black, but today a 'business casual' look is fine. Choose dark, neutral colors such as black, brown, navy or gray. If wearing jewelry, choose simple and traditional pieces.

2. Print the eulogy with large type or line-and-a-half spacing; it's easier on the eyes.

3. Practice! Sure, you'll feel foolish reciting the eulogy out loud in an empty room, but reading it aloud you will start to own the words—allowing you to see how it sounds, develop the right inflections, pauses, etc. Trust me about this. In fact….

4. Read it aloud at least five times. You may realize certain parts needs to be worked on or cut. Does it drag in places? Does it need another story? By the fifth time, you will start to develop a sense of confidence in your goodbye.

5. Coordinate with other speakers. This ensures that there is a flow to the service.

6. Be gracious. Greet your audience before the service. Once you realize this speech really isn't about you (get over yourself already!) it frees you up to bond with the audience. When you stand behind the podium and make eye contact––and you *should* make eye contact —they will not be a nameless mass. They will be people you know sharing a moment.

7. Take a deep breath as you approach the podium—it will center you. It's natural for your adrenalin to be high, but we rush when we're nervous—depriving our words of their rhythm and beauty. Speaking in measured tones, you'll give the audience time to digest your thoughts.

8. Be spontaneous. You're in the middle of the eulogy and it's going well. You recall a story. Diverging from your written text might seem foolish after so much practice, but it might well enhance the eulogy—there is something powerful about the unplanned honesty of that moment. You can always find your way back to printed text.

9. Checklist of necessary items: water, tissue, list of attendees, hard copy of speech. In fact, make several copies. If you do your job well—and you will—people may ask for copies of your remembrance. You may wish to make a gift of your eulogy to close survivors.

Readings For Remembrance

———————◆◆◆◆◆———————

Poets are good at crystallizing big emotions into small spaces. Need a few plifting words? Poach a poem or proverb. Somewhere in heaven Kahlil Gibran will blush for the billionth time.

And ever has it been that love knows not of its own depth until the hour of separation.

— Kahlil Gibran

I am not dead. I have only become inhuman. That is to say, undressed myself of laughable prides and infirmities, but not as a man undresses to creep into bed, but like an athlete stripping for the race. The delicate ravel of nerves that made me a measurer of certain fictions called good and evil, that made me contract with pain and expand with pleasure, fussily adjusted like a little electroscope, that's gone it's true. (I never miss it, if the universe does. How easily replaced!) But all the rest is heightened, widened, set free. I admired the beauty while I was human. Now I am part of the beauty. I wander in the air being mostly gas and water, and flow in the ocean. Touch you and Asia at the same

40

moment. I have a hand in the sunrises and the glow of this grass.
I left the light precipitate of ashes to Earth for a love-token.

— *Robinson Jeffers*

Tears water our growth.

— *William Shakespeare*

The ripest fruit falls first.

— *Shakespeare, Richard II*

His life was gentle, and the elements
So mixed in him, that Nature might stand up
And say to all the world, "This was a man!"

— *Shakespeare, Julius Caesar*

How cracks a noble heart—good night, sweet prince;
And flights of angels sing thee to thy rest.

— *Shakespeare, Hamlet*

Give sorrow words;
The grief that does not speak whispers the overfraught heart
and bids it break.

— *Shakespeare, Macbeth*

When you were born
You cried and the world rejoiced
Live your life in a manner that when you die
The world cries and you rejoice

— Native American proverb

Death ends a life, not a relationship.

— Jack Lemmon

For life and death are one, even as the river and the sea are one.

— Kahlil Gibran

Those things that hurt, instruct.

— Benjamin Franklin

Every exit is an entry somewhere else.

—Tom Stoppard

"I answer the heroic question 'Death, where is thy sting?' with 'It is here in my heart and mind and memories."

— Maya Angelou

Every man dies. Not every man really lives.

— Braveheart

Nature's first green is gold,

Her hardest hue to hold.

Her early leaf's a flower;

But only so an hour.

Then leaf subsides to leaf,

So Eden sank to grief,

So dawn goes down to day

Nothing gold can stay

— *Robert Frost, "Nothing Gold Can Stay"*

People like us, who believe in physics, know that the distinction between past, present, and future is only a stubbornly persistent illusion.

— *Albert Einstein, on the illusion of death*

"Drink to me"

— *Pablo Piccaso's last words*

Songs of Remembrance

Music is the language of the soul. A song is a suitable way to follow up your eulogy and conclude the service or memorial. That said, this is neither the time for "When the Saints Come Marching In" nor a funeral dirge. (Nor, ahem, "Stairway to

Heaven.") Here are a few popular options—though perhaps the deceased's favorite tune might work best.

"Amazing Grace" by numerous artists
"Tears in Heaven" by Eric Clapton
"Knocking on Heaven's Door" by Bob Dylan
"Seasons of Love" from *Rent* soundtrack
"Candle in the Wind" by Elton John
"Morning Has Broken" by Cat Stevens

7 Great Goodbyes

———————•▪●◆●▪•———————

Father or mother, colleague of friend, mentor or muse—the range of farewells can be as dramatic, inspiring, and diverse as the relationships we leave behind.

Here are seven great goodbyes. Some for the famous, some for those who toiled outside the spotlight—but what they all have in common is someone spoke exceptionally well about them.

Read these eulogies for inspiration. Read them for revelation. Read them for possibility and potential: A great eulogy is like a well-lived life—it makes us want to live our own lives with greater abandon.

Bette Davis (1908-1989)

By James Woods, colleague and longtime admirer
Delivered at Memorial Service, November 2, 1989
Warner Bros. Soundstage 18, Hollywood

As a child, I remember reading about The Pony Express, and it filled me with a sense of wonder—these brave young men who rode across the country, at great danger to their lives and well being, to deliver the mail across the United States at a time when it was mostly the territories. The first thing I thought was not how could they have done that, but *why*? Why would they have risked their lives and put themselves in such enormous peril in hostile territory? For what possible personal reward could they have done such an awesome deed?

It was only 20 years later when I was part of the Hollywood studio system that I realized I was on familiar territory.

And it was only when I first saw *Now Voyager* that I saw what real acting was. I was a young man, an actor in New York, with a lot of time on my hands and very little money—but I still had my student I.D. card, so I became a member of the Museum of Modern Art at a reduced rate. They were having a Hal Wallis film retrospective that day, and one of the films they showed was *Now Voyager.* I remember sitting in the dark theater, and seeing a pair of shoes come onto the staircase—and for some reason my heart broke. I sensed there was a person of deep sadness who was about to fill my consciousness. And the camera tilted up and there was Bette Davis, and she was so full of sadness and despair. Her heart was so nakedly broken that I almost had to advert my eyes.

She presented a glimpse into the human soul I thought I had no right to see. At that moment, I understood the awesome power of creative genius. I understood that even an actor could be on par with an Albert Schweitzer or a Vincent Van Gogh, that there was the same kind of hunger and yearning in this performance of naked human emotions. Or in those young men who risked their lives for some ideal or glimpse of the horizon, that I read about in a book as a child.

Another moment: Miss Davis, and Paul Henried are on the side of the stage and she tries to explain what the moment of love that they've had means to her. She talks about a banquet and how there are crumbs left on a table, and if she just had those crumbs her life would be fulfilled.

As an actor, I think about what those words must have looked like on a printed page. I would have looked at them and retired from the profession. I would have said there's no way you can stage this kind of thing, people don't talk this way... But I watched Bette Davis do the scene and I understood the hunger of the human soul for love. What kind of courage does it take to open one's soul that deeply? She played it so ferociously, like a mother lion devouring her kill to protect and feed her young. She did it with such abandon, such need, that I knew there was some higher power at work which compelled her to rip this scene apart.

Some years after that I had the honor of working with her. We were working on a film called *The Disappearance of Aimee*—a period picture, so we were all in heavy costumes and make-up. It was easily 110 degrees every day. We were working far from home and it was a rather tense shoot. On the third day Miss Davis came on the set.

There were about a thousand extras in the big auditorium. They were working for a boxed lunch, under hot lights, for a chance to see other actors and Miss Davis. There was a moment when one of the other actors was being—I don't want to make a judgment—but a little *difficult*. And Miss Davis for all her reputation was being gentle as a lamb. So when one of the other actors had quarantined herself in her trailer, Miss Davis said, "I think I'll go entertain the troops. And she got up and proceeded to do a Bette Davis imitation.

God rest her soul, she wasn't very good at doing it.

She said, I never really did this in the film, but I'll do it anyway: *Petah, Petah, Petah.*

And there she was, the eminent trooper. They laughed, they applauded and they stepped right into her heart in that beautiful way that she had many people do— quickly and smoothly.

Later, I said to her, "Miss Davis, I don't comprehend your remarkable patience. Don't you ever get a little angered by other actors, and I wonder, how do you handle it?"

She said, "Well, first of all you have to have respect for any part, even if it's dreadful, and in any case it's really irrelevant because I'm sure she'll be dead in five years either by her own hand or somebody else's." She was eating a kosher dill pickle as she said that, and she never missed a beat.

Years later, Life magazine approached me and said, "You have been chosen by Miss Davis to be the actor she'd most like to be photographed with, as the great stars of 1939 pose with some new young actors." I was honored she chose me.

So we were posing for Greg Gorman, and she looked great— with the same presence she always had and a little bit more. I said, "Miss Davis is it okay if I…"

And she said, "Oh, I think after all these years you can probably call me Bette."

I couldn't figure out what had accelerated her time process—I always had a sense that it would take at least a couple of decades to get to that point. Maybe she was softening a bit. The years wore on and somehow it had never really rolled off the tongue.

Greg Gorman said, "If you would sit there, and Miss Davis, could you just put your hand on his shoulder."

She looks over to him and says, "I think *not.*"

"Is there a problem?"

"This young man is betrothed, I don't want to cause any problems."

Greg came over to me and said, "She's kidding right?" And I said, "No. I grew up in Rhode Island and she's from Connecticut. She knows one woman does not paw another woman's man."

Greg says, "But she is quite a bit older. I don't think she's a threat."

"Well, *she* thinks she's a threat and I have to tell you, there's quite a bit of woman there. I think probably Miss Davis will always be a threat in that area."

A great woman has a power to move and to pain and to beguile, and she's always been aware of that. But eventually she put her hand on my shoulder and we got the shot. It was okay because she was seduced into it. She wasn't responsible.

I think the great power of Bette Davis was she always knew who she was. She had an obligation to herself and her audience. When you think of what she was compelled to do, the power she put on the screen, the fact that she took upon herself a much greater task—in a battle that took place on this very lot in Glendale, years before Gloria Steinem was in a bunny suit and I say that with all due respect... the fact is that Bette Davis put herself on the line when she just didn't have to. She fought for woman's rights when she was such a big star that she didn't need to carry that extra burden. But she planted a seed that now, decades later, sees a woman as head of a studio on this very lot. And she lies up at Forest Lawn looking down at the studio and she knows that are all here and we love her.

I think of the contribution she has made to what JD Salinger referred to as 'the fat lady in the fourth row.' In *Franny and Zoë*, Franny asks Zoë, "Why do you act?" And he says, "Because I have a secret communion. I have things in my soul that I have to do."

To communicate this makes no difference if there's not someone to listen. But out there, somewhere in the fourth row, there's the fat lady and she sits alone because she has no one in her life. She looks up at the screen and she says, "I thought only I felt like that." I don't think there's a frame of film on this face of the earth where there isn't someone, somewhere who looks up and says, "I thought only I felt that."

For all of us who will be there some day and for those who are there now, I guarantee that up in heaven somewhere they are saying, "Fasten your seat belts, it's going to be a bumpy eternity."

Commentary: That's got to be one of the greatest closing lines. The entire eulogy is remarkable for how personal it is, despite the fact that Mr. Woods knew Ms. Davis only professionally. Aside from hitting all seven keystones, what makes it so compelling is that is does what a good screenplay does: zoom in and out, going from big scenes to intimate, philosophical observations—while giving us a character study. Note how we get a sense of Bette Davis and James Woods; great eulogies are as telling about the person behind the podium as the person in the casket. Very, very well done.

Bob Fosse (1927-1987)

By Neil Simon, collaborator and longtime friend
Delivered at Memorial Service, October 30, 1987,
The Palace Theater, New York City

The first time I met Bob Fosse, a real estate agent was taking me through an apartment I was interested in renting. As I came out of the bedroom into the living room, Bob Fosse and another agent were going from the living room to the bedroom. It was one of those Hollywood 'meet cute' situations. We met and instantly fell in love. It lasted almost thirty years. We had our fights, our squabbles, our reconciliations and we even had our children together… Well, at least they were born a few months apart.

To talk about Bob Fosse as a great director and choreographer is almost superfluous at this gathering. You don't have to tell anyone Babe Ruth was a great hitter. Bob Fosse the man, interested me every bit as much as Bob Fosse, the talent.

A few months ago I started to make notes on a play I wanted to write called *The Hampton Boys*. It was about and based on my impressions of Bob Fosse. When I first started writing plays, a first rate producer once told me, never start with story, always begin with good characters. You couldn't find a better one than Bob... the play concerned a man who was celebrating his 50th birthday—that's Bob, and he decides to invite his ten best male friends out to East Hampton on a bitter cold day in February, to a rather run down rented house, short on heat and amenities, without a phone or television, and have them spend the weekend together, while the Fosse character instigated fights, made them play truth games (that he loved so much), each man getting as his roommate the one man he liked the least... and by Sunday night, when everyone was ready to leave, they had not only had a harrowing experience, but they felt, in some measure, they all had made a breakthrough in their preconceived ideas of each other ... and they left not only closer in their friendships, but with a new awareness even of themselves. That's what Bob could do to you: He could put you through the ringer, and make you test yourself to the limit, because that's what he was always doing to himself. He was one of those people that you had to gear yourself up to be with because you always wanted to be at your best. If you were going to have lunch with him, you had to go out and have lunch someplace else first, just to break in your conversation.

When I heard of his passing, which I don't think any of us believes yet, my mind wandered back to all the times I spent and worked with him, and my biggest regret is that in these last few years, there wasn't enough of that time spent together. And to share this time and my thoughts today, I started to make a list of the most vivid and memorable times I spent with Bob... It's my Ten Best Bob Fosse list.

1) A day in Philadelphia when we were trying out *Little Me*... A terrific song, *Real Live Girl* just wasn't working as it should. Bob disappeared for the day, and that night he called me, Cy Coleman, Carolyn Leigh, Cy Feuer and Ernie Martin into an empty rehearsal studio. There was, as I recall, just a pianist, Bob, and a few props. And Bob proceeded to do the new version of the song, as fourteen soldiers would be doing it. Bob sang and danced not as one person, but as fourteen, making them all so vivid and clear and different, that you didn't know which guy you liked best. They were all funny and some of them were touching. I think I said to Cy Feuer, "Wow. We've got a great cast"... Needless to say, the number became a show stopper.

2) In that same show, Bob and I were sitting together in the second row at the Erlanger Theatre watching a run through. At the end of the performance, the sound of two women in the back of the house applauding. It was Gwen and my wife, Joan, both in full pregnancy. The show and the babies opened just about the same time. I

am happy to say that today, Nicole Fosse and Nancy Simon remain the best of friends.

3) A day of auditions, either for *Charity* or *Little Me*… It was the dancers call and there were easily two hundred dancers to see that day. Bob sat on a stool at the center of the stage, his back to the orchestra seats where I was sitting alone, watching. Each dancer would put his or her dance bag at the side of the stage, then when called by name, would simply come out, do a long run, a leap, a twist and a jump in the air. Maybe more, but not much… And Bob would either say, and always graciously, "Please stand with the group on the right" or, "Thank you very, very much"… After about a hundred dancers had leapt across the stage, one very attractive but very nervous young lady came out, prepared and then did her run, leap, twist and jump and landed with a great smile on her face, looking at Bob for approval and a contract. Bob said, again graciously, "Thank you very much." The girl stood stunned. She didn't move, literally, for minutes. There was dead silence in the theater. She walked over quietly, picked up her dance bag and said to Bob, "No one ever says thank you to me"—and proceeded to pummel Bob with her heavy dance bag, hitting him so hard, she knocked him off the stool. Two stage hands pulled her

away into the wings. Bob got back on the stool, smoothed back his hair and said, "Ladies, no more dance bags on stage, please."

4) The opening night of *Little Me* in New York. I was standing with Bob and Cy Coleman at the back of the house… and Sid Caesar, who otherwise gave a brilliant performance, coughed on each of his first three laugh lines – causing, obviously, no one to laugh on his first three laugh lines. I looked at Cy, Cy looked at me and then we both looked at Bob. Bob very simply put his arms down at his sides, closed his eyes, and fell backwards, every part of his body hitting the floor simultaneously—a perfect Ten at any Olympics. He hardly moved on the floor, except to moan very quietly. And then a few minutes later, a very hostile and inebriated man got out of his seat, walked up the aisle on his way to the men's room, turned to us and said angrily, "This is the worst goddamned show I've seen since *My Fair Lady*"… Bob laughed until he cried.

5) Playing croquet on a bumpy lawn at his house in the Hamptons. Bob was the most notorious and blatant cheater I ever say. The wonderful thing is, he never did anything sneaky or surreptitious. If you were winning, he would simply kick your ball into the bushes in full

view of everyone. If your ball was heading into the wire hold for the winning shot, he would simply pick up the wire before your ball got through it and announce "Lunch" ... Or sometimes he would just pick up the wire and the wicket and just place it an inch away form wherever his ball was. And then he'd smile and say, "What's wrong?" His philosophy was that what he was doing was right. They just forgot to write, "Cheating allowed" into the rule book.

6) Bob's appreciation for the written word. I loved watching his face when I brought in new pages for a scene that needed reworking. He'd put on the glasses that dangled on a strap around his neck, read them and then throw back his head and laugh and say, "Gee, Doc. That's really great." And then add, "Would you like to choreograph the next number?"

7) A night in early September in the Hamptons, when the autumn chill was first in the air and the sunsets were more glittering than ever. Gwen and Joan did the cooking and Bob and I and the kids played touch football in the back of the house. If his team was losing by 31 points, he would grab the ball out of my hand, run for a touchdown and say, "Touchdowns now count for 32 points." We had lobster, corn on the cob and

cold wine, and that's all there was to it, but it's a day I can never get out of my head.

8) Watching him make acceptance speeches for all the awards he won. He *never* said a wrong word.

9) His birthday was June 23rd and mine was July 4th. He was eleven days older than me and it was a constant source of kidding. I'd say things like, "I always look up to you, Bob, and want to be just like you when I get to be your age" … or when he came into a room, I'd get up and give him my seat. I'd say, "It's okay, Bob. I understand. The legs are the first things that go." And he'd say to me, "In the first eleven days of my life before you were born, I had more girls that you'd ever have in all your life."

10) One of the last memories was a party Bob gave out at Quogue about a year ago for the entire company of the new *Sweet Charity*. It was crowded with dancers and actors and was, like all Fosse parties, fun and games. He and I played each other ping pong and the winner was to be designated the youngest forever. He and I finally sat down alone over a glass of wine and reminisced about our lives. He looked at me with a big smile on his face and said to me so sweetly and sincerely, "It was

great, wasn't it?" And Bob won the game. He'll be the youngest forever.

Commentary: Having breathed new life into the Broadway comedy, Neil Simon thought he might do the same with eulogies—droll, with a twist. His Top 10 List neatly updates the genre while giving us a Fosse retrospective: uber-talented director and choreographer, loving husband and father, loveable cheater and womanizer, charming host. Simon teases out these roles with a light touch. (From favorite songs to worst dates, Simon's Top 10 format also reflects our tendency to categorize our lives.) As for the one-liners? Laughter isn't just the adhesive agent of their friendship; it also allows us, the audience to breath a collective sigh of joyful recognition when we need it most.

Colonel Don Conroy ("The Great Santini")

By Pat Conroy, son
Delivered at Funeral, May 14, 1998
Beauford, South Carolina

The children of fighter pilots tell different stories than other kids do. None of our fathers can write a will or sell a life insurance policy or fill out a prescription or administer a flu shot or explain what a poet meant. We tell of fathers who land on aircraft carriers at pitch-black night with the wind howling out of the China Sea. Our fathers wiped out aircraft batteries in the Philippines and set Japanese soldiers on fire when they made the mistake of trying to overwhelm our troops on the ground.

Your Dads ran the barber shops and worked at the post office and delivered the packages on time and sold the cars, while our Dads were blowing up fuel depots near Seoul, were providing extraordinarily courageous close air support to the beleaguered Marines at the Chosin Reservoir, and who once turned the Naktong River red with blood of a retreating North Korean battalion.

We tell of men who made widows of the wives of our nations' enemies and who made orphans out of all their children. You don't like war or violence? Or napalm? Or rockets? Or cannons or death rained down from the sky? Then let's talk about your fathers, not ours. When we talk about the aviators who raised us and the Marines who loved us, we can look you in the eye and say, "You would not like to have been America's enemies when our fathers passed overhead." We were raised by the men who made the United States of America the safest country on earth in the bloodiest century in all recorded history. Our fathers made sacred those strange, singing names of battlefields across the Pacific: Guadalcanal, Iwo Jima, Okinawa, the Chosin Reservoir, Khe Sanh and a thousand more. We grew up attending the funerals of Marines slain in these battles. Your fathers made communities like Beaufort decent and prosperous and functional; our fathers made the world safe for democracy.

We have gathered here today to celebrate the amazing and storied life of Col. Donald Conroy who modestly called himself by his *nom de guerre*, The Great Santini. There should be no sorrow at this funeral because The Great Santini lived life at full throttle, moved always in the fast lanes, gunned every engine, teetered on every edge, seized every moment and shook it like a terrier shaking a rat. He did not know what moderation was or where you'd go to look for it.

Donald Conroy is the only person I have ever known whose self-esteem was absolutely unassailable. There was not one thing about himself that my father did not like, nor was there one thing about himself that he would change. He simply adored the man he was and walked with perfect confidence through every encounter in his life. Dad wished everyone could be just like him. His stubbornness was an art form. The Great Santini did what he did, when he wanted to do it, and woe to the man who got in his way.

Once I introduced my father before he gave a speech to an Atlanta audience. I said at the end of the introduction, "My father decided to go into the Marine Corps on the day he discovered his IQ was the temperature of this room".

My father rose to the podium, stared down at the audience, and said without skipping a beat, "My God, it's hot in here! It must be at least 180 degrees".

Here is how my father appeared to me as a boy. He came from a race of giants and demi-gods from a mythical land known as Chicago. He married the most beautiful girl ever to come crawling out of the poor and lowborn south, and there were times when I thought we were being raised by Zeus and Athena.

After Happy Hour my father would drive his car home at a hundred miles an hour to see his wife and seven children. He would get out of his car, a strapping flight jacketed matinee idol, and walk toward his house, his knuckles dragging along the ground, his shoes stepping on and killing small animals in his slouching amble toward the home place. My sister, Carol, stationed at the door, would call out, "Godzilla's home!" and we seven children would scamper toward the door to watch his entry. The door would be flung open and the strongest Marine aviator on earth would shout, "Stand by for a fighter pilot!"

He would then line his seven kids up against the wall and say, "Who's the greatest of them all?"

"You are, O Great Santini, you are."

"Who knows all, sees all, and hears all?"

"You do, O Great Santini, you do."

We were not in the middle of a normal childhood, yet none of us were sure since it was the only childhood we would ever have. For all we knew other men were coming home and shouting to their families, "Stand by for a pharmacist," or "Stand by for a chiropractor".

In the old, bewildered world of children we knew we were in the presence of a fabulous, overwhelming personality; but had no idea we were being raised by a genius of his own myth-making. My mother always told me that my father had reminded her of Rhett Butler on the day they met and everyone who ever knew our mother conjured up the lovely, coquettish image of Scarlet O'Hara.

Let me give you my father the warrior in full battle array. The Great Santini is catapulted off the deck of the aircraft carrier, Sicily. His Black Sheep squadron is the first to reach the Korean Theater and American ground troops had been getting torn up by North Korean regulars. Let me do it in his voice: "We didn't even have a map of Korea. Not zip. We just headed toward the sound of artillery firing along the Naktong River. They told us to keep the North Koreans on their side of the Naktong. Air power hadn't been a factor until we got there that day. I radioed to Bill Lundin I was his wingman. 'There they are. Let's go get'em.' So we did."

I was interviewing Dad so I asked, "how do you know you got them?"

"Easy," The Great Santini said. "They were running—it's a good sign when you see the enemy running. There was another good sign."

"What was that, Dad?"

"They were on fire."

This is the world in which my father lived deeply. I had no knowledge of it as a child. When I was writing the book *The Great Santini*, they told me at Marine Headquarters that Don

Conroy was at one time one of the most decorated aviators in the Marine Corps. I did not know he had won a single medal. When his children gathered together to write his obituary, not one of us knew of any medal he had won, but he had won a slew of them.

When he flew back toward the carrier that day, he received a call from an Army Colonel on the ground who had witnessed the route of the North Koreans across the river. "Could you go pass over the troops fifty miles south of here? They've been catching hell for a week or more. It'd do them good to know you flyboys are around."

He flew those fifty miles and came over a mountain and saw a thousand troops lumbered down in foxholes. He and Bill Lundin went in low so these troops could read the insignias and know the American aviators had entered the fray. My father said, "Thousands of guys came screaming out of their foxholes, son. It sounded like a world series game. I got goose pimples in the cockpit. Get goose pimples telling it forty-eight years later. I dipped my wings, waved to the guys. The roar they let out. I hear it now. I hear it now."

During the Cuban Missile Crisis, my mother took me out to the air station where we watched Dad's squadron scramble on the runway on their bases at Roosevelt Road and Guantanamo.

In the car as we watched the A-4's take off, my mother began to say the rosary.

"You praying for Dad and his men, Mom?" I asked her.

"No, son. I'm praying for the repose of the souls of the Cuban pilots they're going to kill."

Later I would ask my father what his squadron's mission was during the Missile Crisis. "To clear the air of MIGS over Cuba," he said.

"You think you could've done it?"

The Great Santini answered, "There wouldn't have been a bluebird flying over that island, son."

Now let us turn to the literary of The Great Santini. Some of you may have heard that I had some serious reservations about my father's child-rearing practices. When *The Great Santini* came out, the book roared through my family like a nuclear device. My father hated it; my grandparents hated it; my aunts and uncles hated it; my cousins who adore my father thought I was a psychopath for writing it; and rumor has it that my mother gave it to the judge in her divorce case and said, "It's all there. Everything you need to know."

What changed my father's mind was when Hollywood entered the picture and wanted to make a movie of it. This is when my father said, "What a shame John Wayne is dead. Now there was a man. Only he could've gotten my incredible virility across to the American people."

Orion Pictures did me a favor and sent my father a telegram; "Dear Col. Conroy: We have selected the actor to play you in the coming film. He wants to come to Atlanta to interview you. His name is Truman Capote."

But my father took well to Hollywood and its Byzantine, unspeakable ways. When his movie came out, he began reading Variety on a daily basis. He called the movie a classic the first month of its existence. He claimed that he had a place in the history of film. In February of the following year, he burst into my apartment in Atlanta, as excited as I have ever seen him, and screamed, "Son, you and I were nominated for Academy Awards last night. Your mother didn't get squat".

Ladies and gentlemen, you are attending the funeral of the most famous Marine that ever lived. Dad's life had grandeur, majesty and sweep. We were all caught in the middle of living lives much paler and less daring than The Great Santini's. His was a high stepping, damn-the torpedoes kind of life, and the stick was always set at high throttle. There is not another Marine alive who has not heard of The Great Santini. There's not a fighter pilot alive who does not lift his glass whenever Don Conroy's name is mentioned and give the fighter pilot toast: "Hurrah for the next man to die".

One day last summer, my father asked me to drive him over to Beaufort National Cemetery. He wanted to make sure there were no administrative foul-ups about his plot. I could think of more pleasurable ways to spend the afternoon, but Dad brought new eloquence to the word stubborn. We went into the office and a pretty black woman said that everything was squared away.

My father said, "It'll be the second time I've been buried in this cemetery." The woman and I both looked strangely at Dad. Then he explained, "You ever catch the flick *The Great Santini*? That was me they planted at the end of the movie."

All of you will be part of a very special event today. You will be witnessing the actual burial that has already been filmed in fictional setting. This has never happened in world history. You will be present in a scene that was acted out in film in 1979. You will be in the same town and the same cemetery. Only The Great Santini himself will be different.

In his last weeks my father told me, "I was always your best subject, son. Your career took a nose dive after *The Great Santini* came out". He had become so media savvy that during his last illness he told me not to schedule his funeral on the same day as the Seinfeld Farewell.

The Colonel thought it would hold down the crowd. The Colonel's death was front-page news across the country. CNN announced his passing on the evening news all around the world.

Don Conroy was a simple man and an American hero. His wit was remarkable; his intelligence frightening; and his sophistication next to none. He was a man's man and I would bet he hadn't spend a thousand dollars in his whole life on his wardrobe. He lived out his whole retirement in a two-room efficiency in the Darlington Apartment in Atlanta. He claimed he never spent over a dollar on any piece of furniture he owned. You would believe him if you saw the furniture.

Dad bought a season ticket for himself to Six Flags Over Georgia and would often go there alone to enjoy the rides and hear the children squeal with pleasure. He was a beer drinker who thought wine was for Frenchmen or effete social climbers like his children.

Ah! His children. Here is how God gets a Marine Corps fighter pilot. He sends him seven squirrelly, mealy-mouth children who march in peace demonstrations, wear Birkenstocks, flirt with vegetarianism, invite cross-dressers to dinner and vote for candidates that Dad would line up and shoot. If my father knew how many tears his children had shed since his death, he would be mortally ashamed of us all and begin yelling that he should've been tougher on us all, knocked us into better shape—that he certainly didn't mean to raise a passel of kids so weak and tacky they would cry at his death. Don Conroy was the best uncle I

ever saw, the best brother, the best grandfather, the best friend-
and my God, what a father.

After my mother divorced him and *The Great Santini* was
published, Don Conroy had the best second act I ever saw. He
never was simply a father. This was The Great Santini.

It is time to leave you, Dad. From Carol and Mike and Kathy
and Jim and Tim and especially from Tom. Your kids wanted
to especially thank Katy and Bobby and Willie Harvey who
cared for you heroically. Let us leave you and say goodbye, Dad,
with the passwords that bind all Marines and their wives and
their children forever. The Corps was always the most important
thing.

Semper Fi, Dad
Semper Fi, O Great Santini.

Commentary: Will anyone ever be as good as Mr. Conroy at
eulogizing? Or big-hearted narratives no matter the genre? This
is a master class in remembrance. The keystones are all there, but
what Conroy really excels at is placing his father's life into
context—describing the violent glory of the most famous fighter
pilot in the bloodiest century ever, then zooming in for a close-

up. The close-up reveals no cracks in character or vulnerability. His father is a self-made myth. And so instead of 2AM moments, we get the larger than life moments the Colonel himself liked to tell—about Hollywood, and napalm, and visits to his own gravesite. How personal can you get with a myth? His real name was Don Conroy, but we will always know him as The Great Santini.

Alan Silverman (1955 – 2017)

By Cyrus M. Copeland, close friend
Delivered at Memorial Service, April 23, 2017
New York City

Alan.

I first met Alan Silverman at the Big Apple Ranch—a Saturday night dance hall for gays who wanted to learn country and western dancing, which neither Alan nor I had much interest in. A Jew and a Muslim in a sea of checkered flannel shirts? We really had no business being there. He was dressed in black with a shiny belt buckle and that helmet of silver hair that caught light. We took a spin on the dance floor and I was struck by how gracefully he moved, and by how regal he looked. Our boy Alan had the kind of profile that belongs on money.

I really don't know what I was doing there that night. Except that one meets improbable people by doing improbable things––and Alan was so damn improbable. He was an improbable man who traveled to places and countries where he had no business being. And took a spin. And looked good.

So we became friends. And as the years passed, brothers. He was fun and audacious and cried at every movie we attended--didn't matter if it was a comedy, there was always a small moment of truth which got to him.

And occasionally, he was naughty. One day, I was invited to a party hosted by Anderson Cooper and Rosie O'Donnell, and I asked Alan if he'd like to go. Alas Anderson didn't show that night. But Alan—with that helmet of silver hair, he kind of looks like he could be Anderson's brother, right? And so inevitably someone approached him, shyly, and asked if he was Anderson––and Alan gets a gleam in his eye, shrugs, and says, yes. Followed by: Do you want an autograph?

Word spread that Anderson had finally arrived, and Alan spent the night signing cocktail napkins "Love, Anderson" and posing for pictures with his fans. Then halfway through the party, one of the fans pointed to me and asked if we were boyfriends. We weren't. But here comes that gleam again, and Alan says, yes, I'm his boyfriend—and from there, whenever anyone wanted a picture with Anderson, he insisted I be in it because, dammit, he wasn't going to hide our relationship anymore.

It's a little known but essential fact: Anderson Cooper, by way of Alan Silverman, came out of the closet years before he came out of the closet.

He pushed borders, our boy. He was up for anything, anywhere, especially if it was forbidden. If the State Department strongly advised us not to visit a country, that just meant it would end up on Alan's bucket list. He crossed borders with a spirit of adventure that would make Vasco De Gama bow down in humility, and during the course of his globe-trotting life gave new meaning to the phrase "Wondering Jew" by traveling to over 100 countries.

"Hey Cyrus, I'm headed to Iran next week. Can you teach me a few phrases in Farsi?"

"Wait--you're going to Iran?"

I don't know why I was surprised; he'd just come back from Myanmar which is far more dangerous. So I taught him a few phrases, and sent him off to the 'Axis of Evil.'

What I didn't tell him was that I'd taken a few liberties with my translations—and he left thinking the way to say hello was "*mano beboos.*" It's not. *Mano beboos* actually means "kiss me." So off goes Alan into the Islamic Republic armed with questionable protocols, and a week later he returned with the observation that Iranians were an easily surprised but highly affectionate bunch. It's my belief Alan did more to repair international relations between our two countries than any goodwill ambassador.

We were brothers. We got into each other's hearts, and under each other's skin.

One summer we weren't speaking—I won't bore you with the details, other than to say that if you've got a misunderstanding with your brother, it's best to repair it sooner than not, but I was angry and keeping my distance. Until one day at tea dance, he grabbed my hand and brought it to his lips and kissed it. I marveled that he had the courage to kiss my hand because it takes a lot to kiss someone who is angry. Maybe he was fueled by grace? Or vodka? But he went out on a limb with that kiss. As I look back, it became one of a handful of moments that I've never spoken about or ever mentioned to him, but it held such power for me. The revelation that you could dissolve a knotted heart with a kiss to the hand.

Maybe he was getting me back for sending him to Iran with those kissy instructions? I only recall this: it's very inconvenient being kissed by someone whom you're angry with. But this is the thing about being brothers. You're brothers. You love and argue and get hurt and get kissed.

I feel forlorn right now, not just because I miss my brother but also because it seems there are so few exceptional people left in the world. So few adventurers. And now, one less. The world weighs less without our boy.

And he's not here to kiss our knotted hearts and comfort us. Except that he is—and not just in that way that he lives on in our small kindnesses and willingness to cross borders, although those are undeniably true. But our boy Alan is here. Just yesterday, I was walking the streets of New York and I felt him, walking up Fifth. I felt him walking alongside me, unshackled by the illness that had ravaged his body and made it seem it wasn't really his anymore. He was young again. And vital. And full.

I had a bet with him once: he wasn't sure about the Afterlife, but I was, and bet him a banana split that we would see one another again, and I would collect that banana split at the soda counter in Heaven. I'm pretty sure it was Alan on Fifth. And Alan at the laundromat where I was penning these words, and falling apart in front of the guy running the machines. And Alan here with us right now. Can you guys feel him? You owe me a banana split, Silverman.

Our boy has crossed the ultimate border, and he now knows the answers to the great mystery, and why he was here, what the great gift of his presence was to the world at large—and to each one of us. He knows.

Towards the end, in what I would come to know as the best-worst hours of our friendship, I had the honor of doing Reiki with him. It's a Japanese hands-on energy work. And during the course of one of our sessions, he opened his eyes and looked at me. For maybe five minutes straight. Now, us New Yorkers aren't so comfortable with unfilled silences, but that's how he was talking toward the end. With his eyes. Not even talking—it was a higher form of communication. It was communion. I've never been looked at so long without words. It was a new way of being in these difficult days. A new honesty brought by this terrible disease which stripped him and dispensed with mobility but delivered clarity. Alan seemed so clarified to me.

He brought such grace to the way he lived and died.

You all knew him. He knew you. We had the deep pleasure of knowing and being known and seen by an extraordinary man.

He had a gleam in his eye.

He had a taste for the horizon.

He did good work in the world with Peace Corps, the United Nations, and UNICEF.

He blazed like a comet through our lives.

He left a solar-sized void in his wake.

He had five languages at his disposal, and took great pleasure in wrapping his tongue around intricate syllables. They say you live as many lives as the languages you speak, but we already knew Alan lived large. Which makes it even more difficult to say goodbye. And *au revoir*. And *adios*. And *adeush*. And *jam ak jam*, which is how you say farewell in Wolof.

And *mano beboos*, which is how you say goodbye in Farsi. It also means, I'm waiting for my banana split.

And finally, and most importantly, our boy gave a master class in love. And here we come to the best part of Alan's life. The undeniably gorgeous part. The part that makes us singletons a little bit jealous. The love he shared with Antonio is kind of iconic to me for how well and deeply they loved one another. I am so heartened by their love. By the way Antonio was Alan's hand and heart towards the end when things got tough. In the most difficult time of Alan's life, in his most fraught hours, there he always was. I've said this before and it's no less true for the repetition: the love they shared is the gold standard.

A few days before he passed, I reiterated this sentiment to Alan––about how well and deeply Antonio loved him. And Alan replied, pointedly, proudly, in a way that felt like he was staking an eternal claim, that he loved his husband just as deeply. He wanted that to go on the record.

And so it is entered.

And it will always be true.

Commentary: Writing Alan's eulogy was a whole lot easier than I thought it would be. It had been months since I picked up a pen, my muses having deserted me, but I'd been thinking about Alan intensely in the days prior to his death. I didn't realize it but my thoughts were gathering electricity, silently marking themselves for inclusion. Alan's eulogy had its own sense of agency. An hour later, the words had arranged themselves on the page—that's only the mildest of exaggerations—and I was decidedly back in the creative flow. "Follow the energy" is classical advice for writers and it's no less true of the eulogy. Putting loss into form means taking charge of a deeply sad experience—harnessing the transformative power of loss through its expression. I'd been creatively barren for months, but the death of a dear friend awoke my own creative pulse and muses. Beginning with Alan's name helped. Saying it out loud grounded me. It still does.

Gilda Radner (1946-1989)

By Alan Zweibel, longtime friend and writing partner
Delivered at Memorial Service, June 1, 1989
Lorimar Studios, Culver City, CA

About fourteen years ago I was hiding behind a potted plant and this girl asked if I could help her be a parakeet, and I've been smitten with Gilda ever since. When we met, we were just these two kids in a big city and, because we made each other laugh, people invited us places we never got to go before. And now? Well, I haven't mourned, and I haven't even cried yet, because even though she's dead, I just don't want her to die. I don't know why God makes people and then takes them back while they're still having fun with the life he gave them in the first place. Just like I don't know if I'm supposed to celebrate the fact that Gilda was in my life, or feel cheated that she's not here anymore. But even though her body grew to betray her, spirits just don't die. And that's what Gilda was. Even as an adult, she was still a little girl who believed in fairy tales and that if she said "Bunny Bunny" on the first day of every month, it would bring her love, laughter and peace. Well, Gilda, this is June 1st and if you're in a place where you can't say it, I'll say it for you—"Bunny Bunny" and I hope you're okay. I'm gonna miss you, Gilbert.

Commentary: As Hubert Humphrey's wife frequently reminded him, "Darling, for a speech to be immortal, it need not be interminable." Short works.

FDNY Captain Francis Callahan

By FDNY Captain James Gormley, colleague
Delivered at Memorial Service, December 10, 2001
Lincoln Center, New York City

Captains and lieutenants of the New York City Fire Department share a special relationship with other officers of similar rank. When we meet for the first time we introduce ourselves to each other, we shake hands, we measure each other's resolve and fortitude. At Operations our aggressiveness is based on the trust we share in each other.

Firefighters and their officers share a different, but also special relationship. Officers very literally lead firefighters into harm's way. We go first. If things go badly we are required by our oath and tradition to be the last of our command to leave. Accountability for our men is carved into our heart. Responsibility for our men, their wives and children are in the depth of our soul.

This is why we are here today. Capt. Frank Callahan is the ranking officer killed at the World Trade Center from our firehouse. He leaves last. I cannot say he will be the last to ever leave. We live in a dangerous world, and we put our boots and helmets on every day.

Captains, especially commanding officers of companies in the same quarters, have a unique relationship. We know each other as no else ever will. We are commanding officers of complementary companies. We cannot work successfully without each other. There are not many of us, you could fit us in one fair-sized room. We are not always friends. There is too much at stake, but our respect, and trust in each other, is unquestioned.

Frank Callahan was more than my friend, and to call him brother would not do our relationship justice. Frank was my comrade. It's harder to be a comrade than a friend. It's different than being a brother.

Friends and brothers forgive your mistakes. They are happy to be with you. You can relax and joke with them. You can take your ease with them—tell them tall tales.

Comrades are different. Comrades forgive nothing. They can't. They need you to be better. They keep you sharp. They take your words literally.

When a friend dies we miss them, we regret words unspoken, we remember the love. When a brother dies we grieve for the future without him. His endless possibilities. If your brother doesn't die of old age you might never accept the parting. When a comrade dies we miss them, we regret words unspoken, we remember the love, we grieve the future without them. We are also proud. Proud to have known a good man, a better man than ourselves. We respect the need for him to leave, to rest.

Some people equate camaraderie with being jovial. It is anything but. Camaraderie is sharing hardship. It is shouts and commands, bruises and cuts. It's a sore back and lungs that burn from exertion. It's heat on your neck and a pit in your stomach. It's a grimy handshake and a hug on wet shoulders when we're safe. It's not being asleep when it's your turn on watch. It is trust, it is respect, it is acting honorably.

You hold your comrade up when he can't stand on his own. You breathe for him when his body's forgotten how. It's lifting a man up who loves his wife and children as much as you love your own. Looking them in the eye for the rest of your life and trying to explain, and not being able to. You kiss them for him. It's laying him down gently when his name appears on God's roll call. It's remembering his name. I'll never forget his name. He was just what he was called: Frank. You never had to chase your answer. He said it to your face.

It's at the same time being both amazed and proud that you've known men like him. Looking for your reflection in their image. Seeing it. Knowing you're one of them.

There's a song out of Ireland. A line of it says, "Comrade tread lightly, you're near to a hero's grave." If you ever said that to Frank he would have given you the "look" and pushed past you in the hallway.

Frank was light on his feet but he never tread anywhere lightly. When Frank did something it was like a sharp axe biting into soft fresh pine, with a strong sure stroke. It was done. It was right. It meant something. It was refreshing. It smelled good.

Quite often we discussed history. The successes and failures of political, military and social leadership. The depth and broadness of Frank's historical knowledge was astounding.

I've been told Frank enjoyed a practical joke. We never joked together. Rarely laughed. We never sought out each other's company on days off. We never went golfing or fishing. We never went for a hike in the Shawangunk Mountains together. We were often happier apart than we ever were together because we shared the nightmares of command.

We shared problems. We shared stress. We shared dark thoughts that are now front-page news. Incredulous at the failures of leadership that have borne fruit. We shared the proposition of a time and place where few would dare to go. He went there because it was his turn. He called his wife, Angie, before he received his orders to respond. He told her what was going on. He told her things didn't look good; he told her he loved her.

Historically it is said, "They rode to the sound of the guns":

Capt. Frank Callahan

Lt. John Ginley

Firefighter 1 Gr. Bruce Gary

Firefighter 1 Gr. James Giberson

Firefighter 1 Gr. Michael Otten

Firefighter 1 Gr. Kevin Bracken

Firefighter 1 Gr. Steve Mercado

Firefighter 1 Gr. Michael Roberts

Firefighter 1 Gr. John Marshall

Firefighter 3 Gr. Vincent Morello

Firefighter 3 Gr. Michael Lynch

Firefighter 6 Gr. Michael D'Auria

and Firefighter 2 Gr. Kevin Shea

Kevin, we are joyful that we got you back. Have no guilt. The same goes for the rest of us. I know what you all did, you got your gear on, found a tool, wrote your name or Social Security number in felt tip pen on your arm or a leg, a crisis tattoo in case you got found.

We went down there knowing things could go badly. We stayed until we were exhausted, got three hours sleep and went back again, and again. That's what comrades do. Only luck and circumstance separate us from them.

It is significant that we are in Lincoln Center for the Performing Arts. The first performance here was "West Side Story," the story of this neighborhood. This Act is part of that story. It is more than we can absorb in one lifetime, so the story must be told until it makes sense.

It is poignant because the arts have helped mankind deal with reality since stories were told round the fire and we drew on cave walls. The arts help us exercise our emotions. We are surrounded by art and overwhelmed by our emotions. From the pictures children have drawn for us, the poetry, songs, and banners, to the concerts, plays and operas that we have been invited to attend—use the arts to heal your heart. Exercise your emotions. Feel anger, feel hate, feel love and pride. Run the gamut of your emotions until you settle where you belong, as good honorable men, every inch the equal of our comrades, friends and brothers. That's what they want. That's what your families need. That's what you deserve.

Frank was a trusted leader, a captain. The best commander I've encountered here, or in the military. It was important to him. We both believed captain to be the most important rank in the department. He was forged by his family, his comrades, every officer and firefighter that he ever worked with. He was tempered by his experience.

History, the record of successes and failures of leadership, has caused us to be here. Capt. Frank Callahan did not fail in his leadership. He led his command where they were needed, and he's the last of them to leave. If more of the world's leaders were forged as he was, our world would not be in its current state.

Frank Callahan is a star, a reference point. A defined spot on the map of humanity. Guide on him to navigate the darkness. You will not wander, you will not become lost.

Commentary: A great eulogy, set against the remarkable backdrop of 9/11. Who knew firemen could be so eloquent? Gormley makes me wish I wrote with a splinter of the honesty, depth, and humanity he brings to his comrade—and by extension firemen everywhere. This is not a personal eulogy, but it *is* intimate, poetic, evocative and surprisingly philosophical. "Feel anger, feel hate, feel love and pride. Run the gamut of your emotions until you settle where you belong, as good honorable men…" Here's a man who knows something about the duties of command—and commands of the soul. He knows that giving voice to grief is the first step to healing. And he knows how healing the right words can be in dark times.

Edith Freundlich

By Peter Freundlich, son
Delivered at Funeral, May 30, 2004
Riverside Memorial Chapel, New York City

I think of this as a reunion. My mother first met death a long time ago, at a couple of concentration camps in Germany. The two of them spent every minute together for months, were intimate in unimaginable ways, shared a wooden shelf at night and what little there was to eat, or, more often, went hungry together for days, trudged about in the cold and mud, became a single being almost—and then, finally, parted company. Death decided—to her everlasting amazement—that although it wanted a great many others she knew and loved, and millions more she knew about but had never met, it did not, after all that, want her. This puzzled and angered her forever.

Joy came afterward in her life. She was reunited with my father, and had a fifty-year long marriage to him. To call her devoted is to understate the case. He was the air she breathed; it has been almost literally hard for her to inhale ever since he died ten years ago. And she more than loved, we all more than loved, her wonderful younger brother, who is also gone now. That disappearance was especially terrible for her, coming as it did out of order. She surely expected him to survive her.

God knows she loved my brother Andy and me, and our partners. And she was dizzy about our kids—Keith and Jenny and Jessica and Nick. There are quite a few people in this city her grandchildren themselves don't know from Adam who nonetheless know THEM, thanks to my mother's bragging. They are SO smart, SO sweet, SO funny, SO tall, SO grown up: Think of a good thing and put the word SO in front of it. That was her assessment of her grandchildren.

I could eat them up, is what she used to say. A lot.

The point is that there was great joy in her life ... joy, comfort, love, much hard work, well-tended connections to a world that was no more. Especially in the last few years, that was her central preoccupation: remembering. There seemed to be candles to light every day. Her calendar was clotted with anniversaries. Every conversation with her eventually came down to some tiny crystal-clear recollection of the perished, like a little snowglobe of sadness it helped her to look into.

Oh, and she was vain, with reason, because she was good looking and elegant and knew it. She was very fond of admiration, the more unreserved the better, and of attention, the more undivided the better. And then, especially in the last decade or so, she was terribly easily bruised: A sharp word, a raised voice, a cross look would be enough to wound her for weeks. I was particularly stupid in this regard—dense almost—and spent a lot of time apologizing. My last email from her, a couple of days ago—yes, she mastered email at the age of 80—was yet another acceptance of an apology from me. It said, in its entirety, all in caps and with a bunch of typos, because her keyboard work was rather spotty: "I was hurt but it is all gone now. I love you forever and ever. Your Mom and more."

But Death had extracted an IOU from her almost sixty years ago, and she never forgot that, not for a day. Sometimes I wonder whether so much as an hour went by without the thought popping into her head. Finally, on Friday, after leaving her wondering and waiting for an entire long lifetime, after peeking out from behind every one of the many happinesses she had, after plucking everyone else from just beside her and just behind her, Death at last showed up for her, while she was sleeping in her chair, her TV table in front of her, with a full glass of orange juice on it and a little mosaic of the many pills she took all laid out and ready on a paper towel. Death took her—as she deserved—neatly and politely and respectfully, disturbing nothing else around her, nothing at all, not the juice, not the pills, not the thick pillows behind her in the chair. In that quiet, immaculate room, nothing else was moved, nothing else was touched—except her.

I deeply hope that the settlement of this old debt has brought my mother the peace she should have had long ago. And I hope that she is reunited now with all those—there were so many— with whom she should have spent many more years than she was given the chance by that willful, on-again, off-again figure who first made a claim on her before any of us here were born, and then teased and teased and teased her until just the other day.

Commentary: The highest compliment you can say about a eulogy is that you wish you'd known the subject. I wish I had known Edith Freundlich. Loving, intractable, beholden to the past, she is that genre of Jewish grandmother who is living history—and passing quickly. Having dueted with Death, she knows that remembrance is the way through and so continually brings the past to the present. More than anyone else here, she typifies the spirit of this book, and her eulogy is a fitting conclusion. A great eulogy cannot beat back Death, but it *can* give new meaning to life and this moment.

The Eulogy Awards

I've come across a number of great goodbyes—lauded then lost to history's dustbin. There are notable exceptions: RFK's eulogy for Martin Luther King. Reagan's eulogy for the Challenger Astronauts. Nehru's goodbye to Gandhi. But mostly the art of goodbye has kept a low profile, and that's as it should be. Grieving is not meant for a spotlight.

But grief is no longer the dominant note at memorials—having been replaced by celebration. A new era in remembrance has begun! Gratitude trumps loss. Look no further than Earl Spencer's much admired farewell to Diana, if not exactly a happy farewell, then one which has the uplift of her spirit. And the eulogy—having lingered reticently in curtained-off funeral parlors—is newly confident and ready for its close-up. Let's celebrate this art form! After all, we've got the Emmy Awards, MTV Awards, Country Music Awards, People's Choice Awards, heck, even the American Kennel Club Awards, why not an award for great goodbyes?

In this spirit, I present … The Eulogy Awards, a retrospective romp through 20th and 21st century farewells.

Dim the lights. Drum roll, please.

Best opener: Madonna on Gianni Versace: "I slept in Gianni Versace's bed." Thus ensuring the audience is awake and listening.

Shortest eulogy: Rev. Louis Saunders on Lee Harvey Oswald––one sentence: "Mrs. Oswald tells me her son Lee Harvey was a good boy and that she loved him, and today Lord we commit his spirit to your divine care."

Best eulogy for a fireman: Captain James Gormley on Capt. Frank Callahan: "Some people equate camaraderie with being jovial. It is anything but. Camaraderie is sharing hardship. It is shouts and commands, bruises and cuts. It's a sore back and lungs that burn from exertion. It's heat on your neck and a pit in your stomach. It's a grimy handshake and a hug on wet shoulders when we're safe. It's not being asleep when it's your turn at watch. It is trust, it is respect, it is acting honorably."

Best eulogy for a diva: Ossie Davis on Nina Simone. "'Mississippi. Goddamn.' She needed no other words to describe that situation—the pain and the agony. Oh, she was a great one."

Best Eulogy for a wisecracker: Bob Hope on Jack Benny. "Jack's first love was the violin, which proves once again you always hurt the one you love."

Most unlikely pairing: Teresa Heinz Kerry on Mister Rogers: Not just a strange pairing, but prescient: "He focused on what all of us have in common—the need to feel special, to be accepted for who and what we are. What a gift that was, and how wise we would be to hold onto it in this newly conflicted world of ours, this global neighborhood."

Best way to spin a life: Dan Aykroyd on John Belushi. "What we are talking about here is a good man, and a *bad boy*."

Best eulogy you didn't know was a eulogy: Lincoln's Gettysburg Address—commemorating 7500 fallen soldiers: "Four score and seven years ago …." You know the rest.

Best impromptu eulogy: Robert F. Kennedy on Martin Luther King: Delivered on the back of a flatbed truck, at a campaign pit stop, in racially tense Indianapolis. His aides urged him to skip it. Kennedy insisted—ditching his speech and delivering the finest impromptu eulogy from last century. "What we need in the United States is not division; what we need in the United States is not hatred; not violence or lawlessness; but love and wisdom, and compassion towards one another, and a feeling of justice toward those who still suffer..."

Best eulogy for an anonymous icon: Jack Norris on Bill W., founder of AA: "Bill was no saint. He was an alcoholic and a man of stubborn will and purpose."

First eulogy delivered on a Hollywood sound stage: David Hartman on Bette Davis: "A wise man told me that the most a person can say about his or her life is, "I was here! I mattered!" Well, goodness knows, Bette Davis was here."

Best eulogy for a tough dad: Pat Conroy on Don 'The Great Santini' Conroy: No one tells stories or delivers a eulogy like Conroy, with trademark wit, candor, and lyricism—leaving you sorry you'll never meet his mythic father. "When *The Great Santini* came out, the book roared through my family like a nuclear device. My father hated it. What changed my father's mind was when Hollywood entered the picture and wanted to make a movie of it. This is when my father said, "What a shame John Wayne is dead. Now there was a man. Only he could've gotten my incredible virility across to the American people."

Most surprising use of suicide note: Courtney Love on Kurt Cobain, whose letter was read aloud by Love in lieu of a eulogy.

Best ghostwritten eulogy: President Reagan on Challenger Astronauts: Penned by Peggy Noonan, this send-off was like balm on a searing national wound: "A nation, too, will long feel the loss of her seven sons and daughters, her seven good friends. We can find consolation only in faith, for we know in our hearts that you who flew so high and so proud now make your home beyond the stars, safe in God's promise of eternal life."

Most prolific eulogist: M*A*S*H writer Larry Gelbart: Gregory Peck, Bob Hope, Jack Lemmon, Billy Wilder, Cy Coleman, Milton Berle, and dozens more—all were dispatched to The Great Beyond on Mr. Gelbart's elegiac words.

Best eulogy for Death's ambassador: David Kessler on Elisabeth Kübler-Ross: How do you bid adieu to Death's Goodwill Gal? Not just by telling stories—but also being relaxed enough to address the corpse. Mid-eulogy, he pauses, looks over at Elisabeth and says, "This is actually very unnerving. This is the quietest she has ever been in my presence."

Greatest eulogy for a 9/11 hero: Father Michael Duffy on Father Mychal Judge: One of the best eulogies ever. Period. "Mychal got his uniform on—and I have to say this in case you really think he's perfect—he did take the time to comb and spray his hair. But just for a second. When he got to the World Trade towers, one of the first people he met was Mayor Giuliani. Later, the mayor recounted how he put his hand on Mychal's shoulder and said, "Mychal, please pray for us." And Mychal turned and with that big Irish smile said, "I always do.""

Most watched: Earl Spencer on Princess Diana: Seen by a billion-plus worldwide, Di's send-off is remarkable for its eloquence, its impudence to the royals, and its intimacy. "For all the status, the glamour, the applause, Diana remained a very insecure person at heart, almost childlike in her desire to do good for others so she could release herself from deep feelings of unworthiness of which her eating disorders were merely a symptom."

Most honest: Rev. Howard Moody on Lenny Bruce: "There are three characteristics of his that I recall: his destructiveness, his unbearable moralism, and his unstinting pigheadedness."

Best eulogy for the Dead Poet's Society: Robert Ingersoll on Walt Whitman: Big, poetic, insightful—but also uncommonly personal for a century ago. " I thank him for all the great and splendid words he has said in favor of liberty, in favor of man and woman, in favor of motherhood, in favor of fathers, in favor of children, and I thank him for the brave words that has has said of death ... And so I lay this little wreath on this great man's tomb. I loved him living and I love him still."

Best rhyming eulogy: Robert Hunter on Jerry Garcia: The Grateful Dead lyricist pays tribute in the way he knows best: verse. "Without your melody and taste / to lend an attitude of grace / a lyric is an orphan thing / a hive with neither honey's taste / nor power to truly sting.

Best eulogy for a jock: Bob Costas on Mickey Mantle: "How do you say goodbye to an icon whose Homeric feats endeared him to boys and men everywhere? By being truthful. "He had those dual qualities so seldom seen, exuding dynamism and excitement but at the same time touching your heart—flawed, wounded. ... In the last year, Mickey Mantle finally came to accept and appreciate the distinction between a role model and a hero. The first he often was not, the second he always will be.

Best closer: James Woods on Bette Davis: "Fasten your seatbelt, it's going to be a bumpy eternity."

Made in the USA
San Bernardino, CA
30 May 2019